The Harvey Mackay Network Builder

by
Harvey Mackay

Published by MackayMitchell Envelope Company
2100 Elm Street Southeast
Minneapolis, MN 55414
Manufactured in the United States of America

Includes Table of Contents
ISBN 978-0-578-09128-0

Dedication

This book is dedicated to anyone who ever struggled—
to find a job, buy a house, raise a child, start a business,
finish school, make a sale, invent a product, get ahead,
or make something happen.

Struggling is not a comfortable thing. It involves long
hours of work, worry and wondering. Sometimes we
achieve what we hoped to achieve, sometimes we don't.
Often, the outcome is very different from what we
had planned.

Luckily, there are some benefits to struggling. First,
it helps us grow. Human beings tend to do their best
work when they are overcoming the odds.

Second, we don't have to do it alone.

Wherever we're going, we all need the help of others
to get there. Don't ever be afraid to ask for what you
need. That's what your network is for. That's what your
contact management system (CMS) is for. There are
plenty of people out there waiting and willing to help.
All they ask is that some day, some time, some place,
you find a way to pass it on.

— Harvey Mackay

Acknowledgments

I would like to gratefully acknowledge Lynne Lancaster for her help in putting this guide together. Her marketing know-how, insight, and true professionalism have been invaluable.

Greg Bailey, my executive assistant, is more than my right-hand man. He has been through the trenches with me ... and for me.

Mary Anne Bailey always provides a sharp eye in editing and proofreading.

Also, thanks to my sister, Margie Resnick Blickman, for being my personal editor on all my projects.

Valerie Boyd of BOYDesign produced the ingenious cover design and artwork.

Preface

There we sat, in a crowded stadium watching a heated match at the U.S. Open Tennis Tournament, and my wife, Carol Ann, was talking.

Twenty thousand people and I were there to concentrate. Carol Ann, it seems, was there to network—a skill she has raised to an art over the years. And when you think about it, what better place to meet interesting people than the U.S. Open with its boisterous New York crowd and combustible atmosphere?

However, that day I was in the mood for tennis. I tried a few pointed glances and then a loud "shhhhh." These were blithely ignored.

By then I was so distracted I missed the winning point and the match ended. Carol Ann turned to me, beamed and announced: "That was the best point of the match." Then she went back to talking with her new-found friend.

Eavesdropping, I got the gist of their conversation. Carol Ann had informed her that while we were in New York, we were visiting our daughter, Mimi, who had recently moved there with an advertising degree to try to crack the job market. It seems this woman had played college tennis and now worked for a prominent Madison Avenue ad agency. She was giving Carol Ann all sorts of tips about which firms were good places to work and which were sweat shops, who to talk to, what they looked for in applicants—invaluable information only someone in the know could have possibly provided. In fact, she subsequently invited Mimi, who had also played college tennis, to interview with her firm.

Not long after that visit, Mimi was hired by the same agency. It's a great example of what I firmly believe about networking: To be truly successful in life and in business, you have to have a genuine curiosity about people and a real willingness to work at keeping relationships going over time. That's both a gift and a skill. I can't help you much with the gift part—you either like people or you don't. But I can help you master the skills. Remember, no matter how good you are, you're really only as good as the network you build.

Now, let's get started . . .

Table of Contents

Lesson 1

It's A Chronicle Of Your Life

One of the most important skills I ever learned isn't taught in business school. It's networking. And I wouldn't be a bestselling author or successful business-man today without it. What does a contact manage-ment system (CMS) have to do with literary success? Let me tell you how it changed my life.

Every year, over 600,000 manuscripts make their way to publishers. Of these, about 55,000 get printed, only a handful make it onto the *New York Times* Best Seller list, and just a couple make it to #1.

Because the odds are so great against any one book hit-ting it big, publishers are extremely cautious about the number of books they print in the first edition of a new book. That goes double for business books, and prob-ably triple for first-time unknown authors from the fly-over state of Minnesota. Even though the first printing of a book is critical, publishers will typically print only about 10,000 copies. That way, if the book doesn't make it, the company can more easily cover its losses.

The irony is that, as I quickly learned, the single biggest factor in undermining a new book's success is the lack of them in bookstores. If the books aren't in the stores, people can't buy them. The first printing is vital for another reason, too. If the publisher makes a big commitment to the author up front, they are much more likely to spend the time and money needed to promote the book.

An old friend and successful author, Ken Blanchard, introduced me to William Morrow and Company. I sent Morrow a copy of my manuscript in advance, then started doing my homework to see if I couldn't increase my chances of hitting a 400-foot home run my first time at bat. Using my CMS, I called people all over the country who had any connection whatsoever with publishing. I called printers, editors, agents, lawyers, writers, journalists and owners of publishing companies. From my contacts, I learned the peculiarities of the publishing market...who to talk to, how to negotiate, what to ask for, when to ask for it, what was the market like, virtually every question I could think of.

Based on the information I accumulated, I made a plan. Then came time for my meeting with the Morrow people. I walked into the room and there sat the Chief Executive Officer, the President and the Senior Vice President—three grizzlies meeting an amateur. They had already seen my manuscript and were open to discussion, so things started out on a fairly pleasant note.

The congenial mood in the room lasted just until I mentioned that I wanted them to seriously consider a first printing of my book of 100,000 copies. End of meeting.

Basically, we were on the 16th floor and they invited me to jump. The silence was deafening. They started rustling their papers, closing their books, and checking their watches.

Finally, the Senior Vice President spoke up, "Well, obviously we're not going to have a chance to get together on this, but tell me, Mr. Mackay, who are you to come into this room and ask for a 100,000 hardcover first printing when most of the top books for the past 40 years started out with about 10,000 copies? You're an unknown first-time author. We don't understand it."

I reached down under the table, opened my mini-suitcase and took out my Rolodex file. (This was back in the pre-tech days.) There sat the results of 40 years of disciplined work: 6,500 names. I started going through them. Some countries: France, England, Germany, Israel. Some companies: Pillsbury, General Mills, IBM. "Here's Honeywell," I said, "with 64,000 employees. Here's 3M with 85,000. I know quite a few people in those companies. And I think that if a couple of people buy the book they'll read it and pass it around."

On I went, through some of the movers and shakers I'd met over a lifetime of keeping my file, pointing out those that I thought would be good candidates to ask for endorsements.

Three weeks and three meetings later, they agreed to print an unprecedented 100,000 hardcover books!

For me, that was the culmination of a 40-year journey. Like your book shelf, your CMS is a chronicle of your life. It tells you where you've been, but unlike other monuments to the past, it can also tell you where you're going.

There's almost no direction you can take in business, no decision you can make, that isn't already foreshadowed in your networking file.

One of my favorite sayings is that you must dig your well before you're thirsty. During the years we spend meeting new people, following up with them, tracking their lives, we're really digging a well so that at some time in the future we can quench our thirst— for knowledge, contacts, ideas, assistance, information, whatever we need, whenever we need it.

It's no surprise that my Rolodex was the key to getting my book *published*, because in reality it was the key to getting it *written* in the first place.

When I started writing, I knew I couldn't write a collection of high-brow theories about business. What I wanted to write about was literally in my Rolodex—a lifetime of stories, anecdotes and lessons learned from the people I've known over the years. There's no way you can glance at a Rolodex card without remembering the story behind the person.

People tend to think it's just names and addresses that make the CMS work. They're wrong. The key to this system is having the strengths, weaknesses, interests, family background, hobbies and accomplishments of these people, all at your fingertips. You build that knowledge throughout a lifetime, and I've included my unique system in this book for you to start using right away.

No one on Earth can tell me where he's going to be 10 years from now. You never know, that fellow student from drama class could become your biggest customer or the banker you need to help finance your new business. Twenty years ago, who would have guessed that jailed playwright Vaclav Havel would become president of Czechoslovakia, and later the Czech Republic?

The majority of students graduating from college today don't have the slightest idea what they want to do with their lives. To complicate matters, research tells us that today's college graduate will experience 12 to15 job changes and 3 to 5 career changes in his or her lifetime!

Your CMS is a great way to survive those changes. Whether you're an entrepreneur, in sales, or aiming for another rung on the corporate ladder, you can reach out and tell the whole world about it. You can send out a laser-sharp mailing, you can personalize it, and you can derive a lifetime of confidence knowing that all those people are keeping track of you and your progress.

As a parent, one of the best things I ever did for my kids, and one of the few decisions I've never second-guessed, was to get them started keeping a CMS early in life. All three are out on their own now and I'd estimate they each have at least 2,000 names on file. In fact, my son David is close to hitting the 10,000 mark. The discipline and focus that might have seemed awkward at first has become a lifetime habit, and the contacts they've made give them a super leg up on the competition.

My youngest daughter, Jojo, graduated as a dance major from the University of Michigan. She knew she wanted to work in the field of dance, so she moved to New York City and started pounding the pavement. In her CMS, she came across the name of someone whose kids she had met six years earlier on a family vacation.

She'd been in touch with them a few times over the years, and knew that the father now worked as a producer in New York. She called and reintroduced herself and he offered her several names of people she might talk to. Within a few weeks, she had a job teaching dance to children at a well-known and much respected private school.

If you're wondering about your own network building skills, take the self-quiz in Appendix I to see how you rate.

The late Elliott Jaques was the director of the Institute of Organization and Social Studies at Brunel University in England. He made a career out of studying how executives think (that's *how* they think, not *whether* they think).

One of Jaques' key discoveries was what he called the "time-frame of the individual." While some people find it difficult to plan out what they are going to do today or this week, others function comfortably within time-frames of several months to a year. His work with highly successful executives showed they are able to shape plans that extend far into the future. Some Japanese executives, most notably the late president of Matsushita, can actually conceive of a 200-year corporate plan!

In my opinion, the biggest constant over the lifetime of a career is the relationships we form. Although I have trouble envisioning exactly what my business will be like 10 years from now, I know that whatever I'm doing will be based on the contacts I've already made and those I'm making today. In that way, my CMS serves as a touchstone. It extends my personal time-frame far beyond what my brain could remember. It allows me to keep track of literally hundreds of people who, at some time or another, may become an active part of my life.

There's a great story about the high school baseball coach welcoming his players back in the fall. They'd won two games and lost 21 the year before. He says, "I've got good news and bad news. The good news is you're all back. The bad news? You're all back."

None of us can tell which contacts will be the most interesting or valuable to us as time passes. But with persistence and a genuine desire to stay close to the people we meet, we can expand our relationship time-frame to last a lifetime.

Lesson 2

Always Keep Your Antennae Up

If I were being mugged and had to choose whether to hand over my wallet or my contact management system, it would be no contest. Losing a wallet is inconvenient, scary, expensive, and a pain in the back pocket. But losing my CMS would be devastating. I can replace all my credit cards and I can live without a few dollars. But the information I've gathered over the years—now that's irreplaceable.

How do you do it? Like many great ideas, it's very simple. When you meet someone new, make note of when, where and how you met and anything interesting you learned about that person…hobbies, family data, special interests, etc. As soon as you possibly can (and by this I mean the same day), make an entry in your CMS and save it immediately. You should also note any follow-up contact—a thank you letter, an article sent out, whatever—and when your next contact will occur. That way you can make sure your CMS is working actively for you.

If you don't have a specific reason to contact someone, you might still make a note to follow up in, say, six months. Later, when you get that reminder, you'll find a reason to be in touch. If you have a genuine desire to stay in contact, it's easy. Here are some examples:

You've changed jobs and you want to let people know where they can find you. You might send a formal announcement or a handwritten note with your new business card. You might also want to send a brochure that will interest them, or your new company's annual report.

A friend of mine makes a point of clipping and sending me ideas I can use in speeches. It might be a great quote, a funny story, or even a cartoon.

I'm always grateful for ways to add zing to my talks but I'm even more grateful to know someone's thinking about me. Regardless of what you send, the message is clear: "I value your friendship and I want to stay in touch."

Meeting new people and developing your network doesn't mean much unless you creatively and painstakingly keep the relationship going over time.

It's like the meticulous spender. Everywhere he went he carried a little black notebook where he recorded every single penny he ever spent—tips, parking fees, coffee—you name it, he wrote it down. He only had one problem. He never stopped to add it up.

The key to building a network is keeping track of the small, seemingly insignificant details. As I discussed in my book, *Swim With the Sharks Without Being Eaten Alive*, little things don't mean a lot, they mean everything.

World-class cyclist Greg LeMond is a super example. In the 1989 Tour de France, LeMond entered the final stage of the race trailing the leader by 50 seconds. He estimated that by riding the very best ride of his life he could make up about 30 seconds on the final leg—but that would still leave him 20 seconds behind overall. Somehow, somewhere, he would have to cut an additional 20 seconds off his time.

Sports Illustrated reported that as he raced through the final sprint, LeMond kept his head down and held perfect aerodynamic position, ignoring the screaming Americans crowding the sidelines and looking up only enough to keep himself on course.

He also wore a special aerodynamically designed helmet to cut down on wind resistance against his head. For some unknown reason, his opponent, Laurent Fignon of France, chose to race the final leg without a helmet, ponytail streaming out behind him.

You wouldn't think a small thing like a helmet would make much difference in a road race that takes 23 days to complete and covers 2,025 miles.

The result says it all. Greg LeMond won the Tour de France by a margin of eight seconds!

That kind of success doesn't happen by accident. You can't turn it off and on like a light switch. It has to be a permanent part of your lifestyle. Your CMS has to be used the same way. Once you start having fun with it, your antennae will always be up looking for new ways to use it. Using it becomes a way of life.

An old friend phoned me to tell me about his trip—he just returned from Siberia. Another day, former Notre Dame football coach Lou Holtz called to tell me he had just been elected to the College Football Hall of Fame. After conversations like these, I go to the file and make a note: "Siberia, February 2009," or "Hall of Fame induction, July 2009." I might not talk to that person again for months, but when I do you can bet I'll ask, "How's your skydiving?" or whatever.

Remember, pale ink is better than the most retentive memory. Once you write it down and you know where you can find it again, believe me, you're on your way.

Lesson 3

Consider It An Investment

Throughout your whole life you build a network of people who reflect your values, your beliefs, what you stand for. Think of the hours you spend each day, each week, each month, each year, getting to know people. For some people, making personal contacts requires more time than any other activity in their weekly schedule. I know I spend at least 30 hours a week with customers, vendors, associates, friends and, of course, prospects.

Multiply that by 52 weeks and you're talking about a yearly total of more than *1,500* hours invested in getting to know people.

What becomes of that 1,500-hour investment if I don't follow through? If I don't record it all and put it somewhere safe, how can I be absolutely 100 percent sure I won't forget about it? The answer is simple. That investment is down the drain unless I have a way to organize it and make use of it. The only sure-fire way I've ever found is my CMS.

Nowhere is the ability to develop a network more vital than in Hollywood. A *Newsweek* article described how one firm uses networking and the Hollywood grapevine to create a frenzy of interest over a new script just before they put it up for auction.

"As scripts come in, the agents rev up 'the buzz machine,' putting the word out...that a hot commodity will soon be on the block. If the buzz is loud enough, development execs and producers scramble over one another to get the first look...Eventually, the buzz trickles to the top of the studios...The game used to take days—now it can be over in a matter of hours."

OK, so you're not a Hollywood mogul. What if you only do a little networking each week? The answer is: That's fine—as long as you know how to organize your results so they work for you.

Imagine you're a college student working a summer internship or spending spring semester doing informational interviewing (which is a super idea, by the way). Every day you meet new people. If you meet just two new people a week, that's 104 people by the end of the year.

And that's just the beginning. Before you know it, your CMS will begin to swell with names of people who know you, remember you, and are interested in seeing the direction your career takes.

A prime example of the value of a well-maintained network came in 2002 when the University of Minnesota athletics department, facing budget difficulties, decided to eliminate men's and women's golf and men's gymnastics. How could I, a varsity letter-winning golfer at the U of M, stand by and watch that happen? Of course, I couldn't. So I pored over my CMS and co-chaired a committee which became Save Gopher Sports. The administration assured us that if we could raise $3 million, the three programs would be spared from the budget axe. We connected with former teammates, long-time donors, and folks who just liked golf and gymnastics. To make a long story short, we not only met but exceeded the goal because our base of supporters was staring at us from our contact management systems. As payback, the men's golf team went on that year to win the national championship, a tremendous accomplishment for a northern team that contends with a blanket of snow covering their courses all winter long. Believe me, those students now know the importance of a well-maintained network!

When you're building a network, it isn't important whether you start out big or small. You just have to do it right. Remember, we all start out in life with one thing in common ... we all have the same amount of time in each day. It's just a matter of what we do with it.

Lesson 4

Remembering Doesn't Work

If you're young, you may have to take my word for it.

The fact is, it's embarrassing to be unable to recall a detail about someone you haven't seen for a while. Most of us can barely retain the birthdays and anniversaries of our closest friends, let alone information about all the people who enter our business lives along the way. Some of us are hard-pressed to remember people's names without hoping to recall where they gave that great speech or what volunteer activities they're most proud of. Once you know more than 20 or 50 or 100 people, it's hopeless. Unless you have a system.

Some of the most interesting research on the topic of memory deals with how we use visual cues to remember things. All of us have had the experience of sitting in a final exam unable to recall the answer to the question, but able to picture its exact location on the page in our textbook.

With the right visual cues, our memories are better than we think. Test yourself. Off the top of your head, how many people can you name from your high school graduating class? If you had enough time, I'll bet you could remember a couple dozen. But how many could you recall, in detail, if you had a visual cue—let's say you glanced through your yearbook? Of course you could remember many more, and it wouldn't be just names, faces and ridiculous haircuts. You'd suddenly have access to an amazing mental file of conversations, shared interests, embarrassing moments, and all the other little things of which relationships are made.

Tests made on the brain suggest that we never really forget anything, we just misplace it somehow in that incredible computer that is the human mind. Most of our organizational systems are simply cues to the brain asking it to respond appropriately. Some are physical cues—like the stacks of papers I throw on the floor in front of my office door to remind me what to take home at night.

Others, like the CMS, are verbal and visual clues. When I look at my CMS, I immediately recall much more than what it says in a few lines. I know a whole person, and it's usually someone I'd like to know even better.

I've heard people complain that it's too much work, or that it's somehow artificial to keep notes on people you meet. My response is that for me it's not work, it's fun. And even if it takes a little effort, it's a lot less effort than it would take to replace that information later. There's nothing artificial about using cues to jog your memory.

The benefit of making a few notes on things that interest me about people is that when I meet them again, we can pick up where we left off. You can get to know people so much better if you don't have to begin each conversation with "Where do you work again?" or "Did you tell me you have children?" or "Aren't you involved with the Republican gubernatorial campaign, or was it the Democrats?"

I prefer to start off by saying, "How's it going at Acme Corporation? I read you acquired a widget manufacturing subsidiary. Aren't widgets a specialty of yours?"

It all stems from a very old principle, treating others the way you'd like to be treated yourself. I know how great I feel when I run into somebody who remembers that my daughter and I run marathons together. Believe me, I'd much rather talk about that than the Dow Jones averages or the weather.

Conrad Hilton, founder of the multi-billion dollar hotel empire, was a master at treating people well— and at learning from his mistakes. In his book, *Be My Guest*, he recounts that early in his career, he bought his mother a diamond necklace with profits from one of his first hotel deals. It was an expensive and showy piece, far too elaborate for a lady of her age and elegant taste. Upon receiving it, she burst into tears and left the room. Later she acknowledged it was a wonderful gift but too "outstanding" for her to actually wear.

Hilton goes on to explain: "From that time on I began collecting and storing away little preferences that would make me a better gift giver, both personally and professionally ... I know that when the late and wondrous Gertrude Lawrence was a guest at our Los Angeles hotel some years later, I was tickled that I had overheard her at a theatrical party tell a friend that the tiny white roses in her corsage were her favorite flower. And that gift, of the corsage, thoughtful rather than expensive, made such a warm impression on her that she recommended that same hotel to her close friend Noel Coward."

Caring enough to remember puts you on a special footing with people that is deep, lasting, and ultimately, the most satisfying aspect of your career.

Lesson 5

You Have To Give A Piece Of Your Mind To Get Peace Of Mind

All my life I've hated losing track of people. One of the best things about writing a book was hearing from people I hadn't heard from since I was a kid. I even heard from people who knew my parents but who I'd never met. I remember a very old gentleman in a nursing home who wrote to tell me he had known my father back in the 1930s. He described the kind of man my father had been and said how happy he was to make my acquaintance after all these years.

People like him are irreplaceable. That's why it's so important to have a way to keep track of them. The 80/20 rule is never more true than it is with the CMS. You probably will be actively in touch with only 20 percent of the people listed in your CMS at any given time. For your most important contacts, you need *quality* information that is current, correct and readily accessible.

For the other 80 percent, you need a system that can handle *quantity*. In other words, you want to be able to stay up to date with a large number of people without a lot of cumbersome paperwork or a confusing system that will make you want to avoid the matter entirely.

You want to know that the 80 percent are there to fall back on and to call on when you need them.

Years ago I made an acquisition of another envelope company. The company was left in trust with seven trustees. Everybody and their brother was trying to buy it. It was no secret. They let the whole industry know that the company was for sale. However, seven people had to make the final decision. I went immediately to the CMS file and started to network to see who knew any of those trustees. Could I ask them to make calls to testify in favor of my integrity and character, and to let the trustees know that I would be good for the company?

Over a long period of time, I was successful. I did make the acquisition, and I believe that my CMS was the leg up, the cutting edge, that paved the way. When the vote was taken, I knew I had people in the room who were on my side because I had taken the trouble to learn who the decision makers were, and had asked people to contact them on my behalf. I had also learned that one of the trustees' biggest concerns was that after the company was sold it would be merged to eliminate it as a competitor and people would lose their jobs. Through my network, I was able to reassure the trustees that my word was good and the company would remain intact.

I've heard it said of one of my mentors that he can "see around corners." I think that ability to see beyond your own line of vision is the greatest gift the CMS can give. Almost all of our knowledge and insight comes from other people.

I often hear people repeating the old line that you never know where your next great idea is going to come from. I don't believe it. I know exactly where it is. It's somewhere buried in my CMS, just waiting for me to find it.

Lesson 6

Make It Work For You, Not Against You

If the CMS isn't working at least as hard as you are, there's something wrong.

The same systems don't work for everyone. I certainly learned that with writing.

Most people prefer to use a computer or smartphone. I occasionally still find myself hunched over a yellow legal pad, pen in hand, scratching out an illegible scrawl that very few people in the world are able to translate. Whatever it takes to manage the information until I can get it in usable form.

That's how you need to manage your CMS. Once your system's in place, analyze it. See what works and what doesn't. Identify the parts that are easy, or even fun.

Those are the keepers. Then think about the parts you can't stand. If you're not doing something after 30 days, you certainly won't do it for the next 30 years. And that doesn't mean you've failed, it just means a change in plan.

If I had to name the single characteristic shared by all the truly successful people I've met in my lifetime, I'd have to say it's the ability to create and nurture a network of contacts. But everyone does it differently.

Technology has presented us with a truly remarkable set of tools that make the world a very small place indeed. Consider the story of Mark Zuckerberg, a young billionaire who changed the "face"of networking in a matter of months.

Those who have seen the movie *The Social Network* watched the Facebook phenomenon develop, with humble beginnings from a Harvard dorm room computer to more than 600 million subscribers. Zuckerberg acknowledges that the movie was a fictional representation to build a good story, but doesn't dispute the general facts. He's been compared to Thomas Edison and Alexander Graham Bell for his contributions to communication in the digital age.

Facebook wasn't the first social-media site, but it appealed to a broader audience by making it easy for new subscribers to build their pages and required them to use their real names, not pretend to be someone else.

The applications are unlimited. Some users are merely interested in keeping in touch with family and friends, while protesters in the Egyptian and Tunisian uprisings used Facebook to stay connected throughout the uprisings. Businesses use Facebook to promote their products, offer special deals, and solicit comments. Senator Barack Obama launched a strong social-media campaign which many believe was the main reason for his "status" change to President.

Only you know what approach to network building works best for you. Here are some suggestions:

One young consultant has an ironclad rule that he doesn't leave his office in the evening until he's organized whatever needs to be entered into the CMS. Another friend throws everything he collects for the week into a shoe box near the front door, then empties and sorts it out first thing Monday morning.

A long time vendor to MackayMitchell Envelope Company has another system. She pulls the info of all the people she intends to contact during the upcoming week and places it in little piles on her desk. One pile is for those she wants to visit and another is for those she will telephone. A third pile goes to her assistant who prepares envelopes so then when she has a spare minute during the week she can send handwritten notes.

My CMS is set to remind me about birthdays, anniversaries, and special dates well in advance so that I never miss a big day. You can organize yours to make you look like you have a perfect memory too.

The latest studies done on creativity show that the use of color is a huge factor in both learning and retention. I've applied that idea to my CMS. There are a couple ways to do it. One is to color code groups by function. Customers are highlighted in red, prospects in green, personal friends and relatives in blue, etc.

If I've talked to a friend and updated his or her entry, I always include a date of contact so I can tell at a glance when we were last in touch. If that sounds excessive, try to remember the last time you spoke to everyone you knew. Better to have accurate information.

It doesn't matter how crazy or outlandish your system becomes. As long as it fulfills two criteria: it's fun, and it works.

Lesson 7

Make Connections
The Old-Fashioned Way

John D. Rockefeller once said of interpersonal skills: "I'd pay more for that ability than for any other under the sun."

My father, Jack B. Mackay, possessed a greater gift than anyone else I've ever known for getting along with people. Jack Mackay was the local Associated Press reporter in the days before cell phones, fax machines and computers. The only way he could possibly get the information he needed was to know enough people who would share it with him. As a kid, I was amazed that whenever we walked down the street he could hardly take 10 steps without someone calling out, "Hi, Jack!" I also remember his dog-eared Rolodex file in its prominent place next to the teletype machine. I don't know how he could even read it, but he did, and his career depended on it.

As I was growing up, when I asked my father a question, he didn't always know the answer, but he always knew someone who did. That's a great lesson for a child to learn. You don't have to know everything, as long as you know people who know the things you don't.

27

In my opinion, one of the greatest mistakes you can make when you're just starting your career is being afraid to ask for help. Most so-called "gurus" are downright flattered when someone asks their opinion, on anything—whether they know something about it or not. People love to share their knowledge and opinions. If you've ever been at a cocktail party and happened to mention teenagers, or travel or golf, or dog training, you'll understand what I mean. One of my favorite charities just scored a coup by acquiring, at no charge, the services of a highly paid marketing consultant. When asked why she chose to work with that particular group, she replied, "You were the first ones to ask."

I've used my CMS to make connections for friends, friends of friends, employees, and customers. My kids have benefited, too. When my daughter, Mimi, spent her junior year abroad in Madrid, I wandered through my CMS and found a treasure trove of names of people she could contact. What might have been a siesta year became a fiesta year!

Any type of contact can ultimately contribute toward your long term goals. I received an unexpected invitation to speak to the international sales force of a major corporation. After a little digging, I learned that they had invited me because my speech coach sat next to their special events coordinator one Sunday in church.

When you're making connections with people, they aren't always the most obvious ones. That's why I use a specialized format for organizing information. If all I wrote down was name, address, phone number and place of business, I'd be limited to those kinds of connections. But I like to keep track of the special things—the extra things people do with their lives.

If you were job hunting and asked me for the name of someone in advertising, for example, I could probably respond off the top of my head (on a good day). But if I use my CMS, I can tell you the name of an advertising person who loves tennis like you do, belongs to the same political party, lives in your neighborhood, has a child at your alma mater, comes from your small town . . . you get the picture.

When I first decided to write a book, my writing experience was limited to a few articles in regional magazines. I had a lot of ideas, but didn't have a clue how to organize them into a readable format, let alone how to find anyone to publish them. That was one occasion where my CMS proved invaluable.

After a little searching, I realized I had a number of contacts who could provide me with the help I needed. They weren't necessarily the first people who might spring to mind—authors and the like—but they were people who could help. Without my CMS, I never would have thought of them.

One of them was the proverbial "high school nerd turned success" story. In the years since high school, I've tracked the careers of a lot of people I assumed I might never see again, but in whom I had some spark of interest. One of them was a fellow I'll call Dale. He was your quintessential introvert, perennially on the outside of whatever the popular kids were doing, probably off in his own little world thinking about how he was eventually going to succeed if he survived adolescence. I always liked him, and, even though we didn't have a lot in common, I always made a point of speaking with him when I saw him.

Since graduation, I had probably seen him only four or five times, but we kept in occasional contact through holiday cards, and I enjoyed sending and receiving a brief update.

Thirty-five years later, I found myself in the shoes of the first-time author trying to ensure that my book was going to make it. Digging through my CMS, I spotted a familiar name. It was Dale, and I noted that he had gone into something related to the book business.

I tracked him down, and it turned out that he had become one of the largest wholesale book distributors on the West Coast. I contacted him and he placed an order for 10,000 books, ten times the usual order. When I thanked him he said, "I have always remembered our friendship in high school. It's meant a lot to me."

Lesson 8

Unlock The Secrets Of The Universe

It may sound like I'm exaggerating, but most of the important secrets of the universe can be found in my CMS. Granted, the pyramids don't quite fit, and I never have understood the theory of relativity. But a lot of the *other* important secrets are there, like who gives money to what favorite charity, or who used to work for whom.

You say those don't sound like very exciting secrets? Well, the theory of relativity isn't so exciting either if you don't know how to use it.

There's a man named Barnett Lipton who has made himself both rich and famous by producing spectacles. Not the kind you wear, but the kind you watch. He produced the opening ceremonies at the 1984 Olympics in Los Angeles (remember the 84 pianos?) and went on to do the halftime shows for several Super Bowls, among other things.

When asked what he had in mind for the opening ceremonies at the 1990 U.S. Olympic Festival, Lipton said the audience could expect at least "five wows"— five unforgettable special effects.

I'm crazy about that concept of wowing the audience, whatever the occasion. If you and I could make a sales call or a job interview as exciting as an opening ceremony, we'd win every time. All we need are the "wows," and we probably don't even need five of them.

Lipton competed in a class by himself where every production contained more wows than the last one. Fortunately for us—and unfortunately for our customers—we don't. The last time your customer, or the person sitting across the desk from you in a job interview, experienced something that made them sit up and say "wow" was probably long ago, if it's ever happened at all.

How do we go from humdrum to "wow?" The answer is simple even though most people will never think of it. It's in the CMS.

Barnett Lipton knew the only way to create a fantastic half-time show for the Super Bowl or an Olympic opening ceremony was to know his customer, which in this case was the audience. He knew what they expected and he knew what they *did not expect*—and he fulfilled both. That's exactly the same mission we have in selling.

First, we have to know what the audience *expects*. For a half-time spectacle, it's a zillion bands, a zillion dancers on platforms and a laser light show. For a sales call, it's being on time, well-prepared and knowledgeable about your product, with a sense of humor thrown in.

Second, and this is the part most people ignore, we have to know what the audience *doesn't expect*. Because it's the unexpected that makes us unforgettable.

What the customer doesn't expect is that you'll go the extra mile to make an impression. They don't expect that you'll know about their recent problems with on-time delivery, or that they've added a subsidiary in Tuscaloosa. They certainly don't expect that you've done your home-work on how your company could participate in their new company-wide quality assurance program.

When I was writing my second book, *Beware The Naked Man Who Offers You His Shirt*, I was asked to appear on the Oprah Winfrey Show. One of the main ideas I wanted to get across was how important it is to re-ally know your customer. As a guest, I knew what was expected of me because I'd watched probably a hundred other authors hit the interview circuit and perform the same old tricks. I decided to do the unexpected.

First, I did a computer search on everything written about Oprah over the last several years. Then I made copious notes and tucked them into my briefcase. Imagine her surprise on network television when I reached down under my chair, pulled out a four-foot-long computer printout and proclaimed, "Before we talk about me, Oprah, let's talk about you!"

It was all there. Her childhood, family, education, early career, later successes. She'd been on 62 magazine covers and I could name all of them. It brought the show to a stand-still. These unexpected but welcome "wows" don't come from out of the blue. They come out of your CMS.

All my life I've been a voracious, if unpredictable, reader. I'll read whatever I can get my hands on—especially if it pertains to my business or my customers. As I read, I highlight points of interest and clip out pertinent items. Usually, the greatest ideas are the simplest. I'm looking for the little gem of information that makes me stop and say "wow." And when that gem applies to a customer, a prospect, an associate or a friend—you guessed it, it goes in the CMS. You don't have to write a lot, just a little note to remind you of your big idea. That's where the "wows" come from.

Lesson 9

You Can Improve On Human Nature

An ancient Chinese proverb advises:

If you want one year of prosperity, grow grain.
If you want ten years of prosperity, grow trees.
If you want one hundred years of prosperity, grow people.

Deep down, we all know it's true, yet fear very often keeps us from maximizing our contacts with other people. Fear is a real key. Human beings are full of fears; we procrastinate, we don't trust ourselves, we're afraid that we'll fail.

One of the most brilliant individuals I know, an inventor of medical products, has an office that looks like it was touched by Hurricane Katrina. Papers cover the desks, the tables, the walls and the floor. He even has things taped to the lampshades! When I asked him why he let it get this way he answered, "I'm afraid if I put all this away, I won't be able to find anything!"

In our company, my office is notorious as a sort of organizational Bermuda Triangle. Many things go in, but unless my assistants attack with shovels, nothing ever comes out. That's because I've always been an information junkie. I just can't pass up an intriguing business book, a good article, the latest CD, or anything else that might strike my fancy.

The single exception, the method to my madness, has always been the CMS. For me, it's more than a habit. It's a way of life. If I can keep track of the people and affiliations that are important to me, then I know the rest of the business will fall into place.

The key, of course, is discipline. Whenever I share my philosophies about organizing and using the CMS, I get flack from my sales force. "Why give it away?" they groan. "We've worked so hard, let's keep it to ourselves." My response is always the same. Number one, no matter how well anybody else uses it, we've got a 50-year head start on them. Number two, 90 percent of the people that hear about it will never put it into practice anyway.

In my entire career I have never once heard a successful person say he regretted putting time and energy into keeping his CMS. It's one of the few tools that's absolutely, positively guaranteed to work. Experts on human behavior say that it takes just 30 days of consistent practice to form a new habit. It's amazing to me that so few people are willing to persist in something for 30 days, especially considering the rewards.

Once I had to hire an attorney to negotiate a property deal for me and several limited partners in New York. Anyone who knows anything about New York real estate deals knows that it is a contact business—building inspectors, drain commissioners, construction union bosses, and an endless list of go-betweens.

I insisted that the last two interviews be held in the finalists' own offices. Did I look at their hunting trophies or the oriental rugs on their floors? Was I impressed by how many pictures of handshakes with borough presidents bedecked the walls, or the script on the Juris Doctor degree? No, I asked how large their contact management systems were.

The first attorney boasted a mammoth CMS that spanned every profession and union imaginable, and he knew how to reach them at every hour of the day or night. The second attorney referred me to his assistant, who asked me why I wanted the information. Which one do you think I chose?

One of the greatest human fears is asking for what we really want. If we're not very good at asking, we'll feel foolish and fear we might get turned down. Yet, if we make a science of it, we're afraid of being seen as manipulative.

It all comes down to liking people. I get a real kick out of adding people to my CMS. I might not see someone for five or ten years, but sooner or later they crop up again, and it's always fun to get reacquainted.

One of my favorite quotes on the subject comes from Conrad Hilton. He wrote of his early success, "I do believe in luck. But the kind I believe in has to do with people ... The value of buddies was something you learned in the Army where your life depended on how well a hundred other men carried out their assignments. In the Army you were as good as your buddies ... Later, when I reached the rarefied air of Big Business, I learned to call them 'associates.' The facts remained the same. All my life I have only been as good as my associates, and in them have found my good luck, my fortune."

Lesson 10

Never Say No For The Other Guy

Every three or four months I give myself a treat. I take
a few hours out of the day, shut the door, sit at my desk
and just travel all over the world through my CMS.
I'll call Istanbul or Indianapolis or wherever strikes my
fancy just to say, "Hello, how are you," and it's terrific,
especially when I contact people I haven't talked to for
a while.

Since my children have gotten old enough to grab a
backpack and take off on their own pilgrimages, it's been
great fun to watch them get in touch with old friends
who live in places slightly more exotic than Minneapo-
lis/St. Paul. I would have been far more worried about
some of their travels if they hadn't known they had lists
of names and numbers of people to call in every city
along the way—all gleaned from the CMS.

I decided to cross-reference my CMS by city. That way,
if I know I'm going to Orlando, for example, I can pull
the names of all the people who live there and decide
who to look up when I arrive.

As a lifelong tennis enthusiast, one of my greatest
fantasies was to some day find myself sitting in a center
court box at Wimbledon. Now, for those of you who

are as ignorant about the intricacies of such things as I was, I will tell you that you and I have about as much chance of getting courtside seats at Wimbledon as you do in arranging to borrow the crown jewels. In fact, it may even be harder, since I know who has the crown jewels, but I didn't have a clue who was in possession of those great seats that are mysteriously handed down from generation to generation.

Like most people, I hate revealing my ignorance. But each time I do it, I remind myself that the worst thing I'm going to hear is "no," and even if I hear a "no," I'm going to learn something.

I decided to ask an old friend who had become a banker in London. I figured I had nothing to lose except the long distance charges for the time it took him to quit laughing, so I found his number in my CMS and gave him a call.

After the usual pleasantries and a little hedging, I popped the question. Imagine my surprise when, instead of laughter, I heard silence. Then I heard the magic words, "Maybe we can work something out." It seems his bank was one of the oldest banks in London and had, since time immemorial, held a small block of priceless Wimbledon tickets that it parceled out to "favored" clients.

Lately, the bank's fortunes had declined slightly and they had begun looking for ways to add some influential American companies to their corporate client base. Introductions to those companies might be worth more to the bank's bottom line than the good will they engendered each year handing out tickets to existing customers.

The end of the story shouldn't seem so surprising, but it still amazes me. A search through my CMS provided me with names of friends who I thought might have an interest in banking with a London bank, and several months later, there I sat in my version of the crown jewels—courtside seats at the greatest tennis tournament in the world!

In May 1990, history was made in my home state. When Soviet Premier Mikhail Gorbachev first announced plans to visit the United States, everyone assumed he would visit the old standby, Washington, D.C.

Rudy Perpich, the Governor of Minnesota, hatched the crazy notion that Gorbachev might also like to visit some other parts of the country. So he wrote him a letter. And he asked 70 Russian students on campus at the University of Minnesota to write him letters as well telling him how great it would be for him to see the Heartland.

Perpich asked for the order, risked that he would be turned down, and to everyone's amazement, he got what he wanted. For a day in June, Minnesota turned itself upside down to welcome one of the most influential leaders in modern history!

The moral? Never say no for the other guy. Most people avoid risks their whole life by assuming the other guy is going to say no. You have your whole CMS with all its awesome power right in front of you. All you have to do is ask. I guarantee you, if you get enough nos, you're bound to get a few yesses. So don't say no for anyone. You never know when you'll create for yourself the opportunity of a lifetime.

Harvey's ABCs Of Networking

The alphabet is a great place to start as you build your network—organize your contacts from A to Z. But the alphabet serves another networking purpose: there are 26 lessons that you should learn and remember. Now it's time for the ABCs of networking:

A is for antennae, which should be up every waking moment. Never pass up an opportunity to meet new people.

B is for birthdays. It's always advantageous to know the birthdays of your contacts. You wouldn't believe how much business our sales reps write up when they call on their customers' birthdays.

C is for contact management system. Have your data organized so that you can cross reference entries and find the information you need quickly.

D is for dig your well before you're thirsty.

E is for exchange and expand. When two people exchange dollar bills, each still has only one dollar. But when two people exchange networks, they each have access to two networks.

F is for Facebook and all other social media. These sites open unlimited possibilities for networking. Use them wisely.

G is for gatekeeper. There usually is a trusted assistant trained to block or grant your access. Don't waste their time, and make sure you acknowledge their significant role in reaching the boss.

H is for hearing. Make note of news you hear affecting someone in your network so you can reference it at the appropriate time.

I is for information. You can't (and shouldn't) talk about business all the time. Learn everything you can about your contacts' families, pets, hobbies and interests. Humanize your approach.

J is for job security, which you will always have if you develop a good network.

K is for keeping in touch. If your network is going to work, you have to stay plugged in and keep the wires humming.

L is for lessons. The first real networking school I signed up for after I graduated from college was Toastmasters. Dale Carnegie schools are designed to achieve similar goals.

M is for mentors. In the best of all possible worlds, your role models can become your mentors, helping you, advising you, guiding you, even lending you their network as you build your own.

N is for a network of contacts. A network can enrich your life.

O is for outgoing. Be the first to introduce yourself, lend a hand, or send congratulations for a job well done.

P is for people. You have to love people to be a good networker.

Q is for quality. A large network is worthless unless the people in it can be counted on to answer in an emergency at 2 a.m.

R is for reciprocity. You give; you get. You no give; you no get. If you only do business with people you know and like, you won't be in business very long.

S is for six degrees of separation, the thought that there is a chain of no more than six people that link every person. Someone you know knows someone who knows someone you want to know.

T is for telephone. Landline, cell, internet—this is a critical tool for staying in touch with your network.

U is for urgency. Don't be slow to answer the call, even if you never expect to have your effort repaid.

V is for visibility. You've got to get involved in organizations and groups to get connected, but don't confuse visibility with credibility. You have to give in order to get.

W is not only for whom you know, but also for who knows you?

X is for the extra mile. Your network contacts will go the extra mile for you, and you must be willing to do the same for them.

Y is for yearly check-in. Find a way, even if it's just a holiday card, to stay in touch.

Z is for zip code—do you have plenty represented in your network?

Harvey's Top 10 List Of The Biggest Networking Mistakes

Take it from an old grizzly who's been there and done that. We like to think that with age comes vast experience. Guess where that vast experience came from? That's right.

Until someone invents a Teflon-coated suit, the most penetrating insights come from hindsight.

Is there a bright side? Sure. The more you learn from everyone else's mistakes, the fewer you have to make yourself.

Here are a few goodies:

1. Don't assume the credentials are the power.
As every salesperson knows, the key to the sale is knowing who's got the hammer. Every outfit is different. No organizational chart can tell you who the real decision maker is. The most important decision maker often can be found lurking behind the most inconsequential or incongruent title. You need a network to find out where the power is.

2. Don't confuse visibility with credibility.
Don't join any organization, particularly a religious organization, solely to advance your own interests.

Your motives will be as painfully obvious as a deathbed conversation.

3. **Don't be a *schnorrer*.**
That's Yiddish for people who constantly take a little bit more than they are entitled to. (That's as opposed to a *goniff*, who is an outright thief, and a *nudge*, who is merely annoying. Yiddish provides endless gradations for defining difficult people.) Save your big favor request for the big issues. Keep a running balance in your mind of what you have asked for and what you've delivered, and don't overdraw your account.

4. **Don't say "no" for the other guy.**
Use common sense. It's one thing to make a pest of yourself or to overreach. It's quite another to be afraid to reach out for help when you really need it.

5. **Dance with the one that brung you.**
When someone in your network comes through, don't be a stiff. Dinner, flowers, a box of candy, tickets to a special event, a card, or even a phone call is called for. Remember, these people didn't have to extend themselves for you. But they did. And here's a tip: Be sure to thank the person at the top. No one ever does, because they think he or she hears all day long what a super job their company is doing. A heartfelt "thank you" will be music to their ears. Do it and you'll be remembered.

6. **Don't mistake the company's network for your network**. If you're going to keep your job, your network has to be as good as or better than your own company's. You need:

a. Support and sponsorship in other departments besides your own, so that you're able to jump to another department if yours is downsized or jettisoned.

b. Lines of communication that tell you what's happening in other parts of the company—who's growing, who's shrinking.

c. An outsider's objective view of your company and how industry-wide trends are affecting your role in it.

d. Foreknowledge of what skills are going to be in demand at your company.

e. A backup strategy in case you are let go, i.e., a career network outside the company.

7. **Don't be slow to answer the call**.
There's a call on your answering machine. You know that it's a request for help, and that it's going to take some time and trouble on your part to respond satisfactorily. Do you stall? Do you ignore it? Don't.

8. **It probably isn't just your network that's aging; it's you**. Times change. Your network is only as good as the knowledge and information you can bring to it.

9. **Don't underestimate the value of the personal touch**. Small businesses that survive and prosper know how to network with their customers and prospects by emphasizing a level of personal service and attention that the big businesses can't.

10. **If you don't know, ask. Even if you do know, ask**. Draft a questionnaire and put it where customers can pick it up. Suppliers are also a great source of information. You are their customer, so they have a vested interest in your success. You'd be surprised at the wealth of information they have, if you just tap it.

A small business can develop a network of epic proportions. The small business person can be more creative than a national chain and tailor-make promotions to their target audience.

Harvey's Top 10 List Of The Best Ways To Stay In Touch With Your Network

1. Use the calendar creatively.
Sure, send birthday and anniversary cards, but recognize your network's other special days. Never underestimate the power of a simple thank-you note, remembering a date or a place that's important to a member of your network, or a note of congratulations. Yes, Mom was right. Little things mean everything.

2. Watch for important community events.
Here's another place where you can use your awareness of your network's group affiliations to connect. Let's say your network includes this year's chair of the local Red Cross drive. Attend the annual meeting, or send in your donation—without being asked—in their name. By the way, whenever you donate to an organization or a political campaign, there's an old bit of street wisdom that goes: The more hands it passes through, the more people who know about it.

3. Observe organizational/personal/company changes. Local papers and magazines all have business columns that feature significant new hires and promotions. When one of your network members lands on the list, hand-write a note or make a phone call.

4. **Get wired**.

Make sure your CMS includes e-mail addresses, Twitter accounts, Facebook and LinkedIn info.

5. **Clip and ship**.

You can stay in touch with your network just by reading the paper—newsprint or online. All you have to do is be sufficiently aware of your members' interests to forward an article or a quote occasionally that might interest them.

6. **Use your pit stops constructively**.

There are active members of your network who you won't see from one year to the next. Never neglect them when you're in their area, even if it's just a layover at the airport and you can't visit with them personally or take them to dinner. Be considerate. Call.

7. **When your network is filled with static, you can help clear the air**. Is one member of your network at odds with another? You can be an honest broker and help them resolve their dispute. I won't kid you, this is a high-risk proposition. It's quite possible that one—or both—of them will wind up blaming you. If you've got the personality to do it, go for it. A network should not be viewed just as a tool for your own personal benefit. Used properly, it can work for the benefit of others, and that applies here.

**8. Anyone can call them when they're up.
Remember to call them when they're down**.

One of your network members has lost their job. Now is the time to offer them any help you can in making a new connection. When you need help, it surely lightens the burden to know you have a network of people that you have helped. Once you get into the habit of helping others, it's satisfying in itself without regard to any possible reward.

9. Report any major changes in your situation.

You've been promoted. You've changed companies. You've just joined the Little League or the Junior League or the American League. Tell your old network about your new network. It gives you an opportunity to stay in touch. It gives them an opportunity to expand their networks.

10. Be there.

Sure, you can skip the wedding and send a spoon, but don't. Weddings, confirmations, graduations, school plays, bar mitzvahs, recitals, and the big award. People always remember who was there and who wasn't.

Humanize Your Selling Strategy

At MackayMitchell Envelope Company,
"know your customer" isn't a cliché,
it's the foundation of our business.

(Reprinted with permission for one-time use from Harvard Business Review)

Author's Note: My article was originally published in the Harvard Business Review in March–April 1988. While the core concepts are still valid, the techniques for collecting and storing data have been revolutionized by technology in the past 23 years. As a result, I have updated the text to reflect some of the most dramatic changes. Also, certain marketing illustrations may no longer have the validity they once did. It's not as easy to replace them because marketing trends are simply different today. The reader will get the best benefit from the article by focusing on the attitudes and goals of an informed, people-based approach to selling.

You are sitting in a conference room with your marketing manager and sales staff, engaged in reviewing the account of a key customer. To begin her analysis, the account executive clicks on the customer's file and reads aloud:

"Staunch Republican"

"Midwestern value system"

"Enthusiastic booster of the Boy Scouts"

"Avid stamp collector"

"Procrastinates on major buying decisions … needs strong follow-through"

Of course, the report also includes data on the market position, new product lines, and plans for factory construction of the customer's company. But a sizable portion of the discussion focuses on the customer's personal chemistry and characteristics … and how well the salesperson understands these traits and creatively markets to them. Sound like a peculiar use of management time? For many marketers such a discussion would border on the unorthodox, but companies that ignore such vital and revealing information are at a distinct disadvantage in the marketplace.

Many companies are becoming ever more adept at using segmented marketing strategies. In mere seconds, e-mails, video and print messages can establish instant rapport with a targeted customer. But in the meantime, businesses have lost sight of the need to humanize their selling strategies. Computerized purchase orders, rampant cost analysis, and sophisticated financial modeling have overwhelmed the salesperson-corporate customer relationship.

Envelopes are not a glamorous business. In fact, they are about as drab a commodity as you can imagine—in what is nearly the textbook definition of a mature industry. That means you have to be especially good at differentiating your company if you expect to gain market share. In the envelope industry, MackayMitchell's products are constantly being assaulted by new, sexier, more convenient ways to communicate, like e-notebooks, smart phones, and YouTube. A company's margins can be paper-thin.

Despite these drawbacks, in the past 10 years MackayMitchell Envelope Company has seen its sales volume rise an average 11 percent a year to $100 million, and its market share rise to 4 1/2 percent nationally (pretty good in this fragmented industry; there are approximately 100 envelope companies in the country). MackayMitchell has also become one of the most profitable companies in the industry. We credit our success to one factor more than any other: salesmanship—inspired, energized, superior salesmanship.

For years it was fashionable for U.S. executives with any decent pedigree to sneer at sales, the land of Willy Loman. But today, we are beginning to see a mighty redirection of the resources of the American corporation. Head counts in administration, production, and R&D are dwindling, but sales forces are on the rise.

When IBM announced it would trim its staff by 12,000 by the end of 1987, it simultaneously reassigned 3,000 people to its sales forces. The transformation of Campbell Soup from a gray lady to a leading business innovator is largely attributed to a new marketing strategy that has focused on targeting and selling to sharply defined customer niches.

Former Porsche CEO Peter Schutz, in an interview in *Harvard Business Review,* stressed how much time he spent in the Porsche delivery room talking with customers and learning about their motivations and idiosyncrasies.

At MackayMitchell Envelope we use every means we can think of to exalt selling and salespeople. The parking place just outside the door of the main office is not reserved for the CEO. Above it is this sign:

Reserved for
(we fill in the name)
Salesperson of the Month.

This is our way of declaring to our 500 employees, our visitors, and the world at large that sales are at the very heart of our business.

During speaking engagements at management seminars from Athens to New Delhi, I have talked with operators of myriad other businesses, from truffles and textiles to trucks and high technology. The problems and challenges I have heard described are extraordinarily similar, and most of them turn on a failure to manage selling fundamentals. Use of a few simple tactics and disciplines can alleviate many problems.

Know your customer ... in spades

In a one-hour lunch you can learn everything from a golf handicap to views on the federal deficit, from size of home to favorite vacation spot. "So what?" I've heard people say. "It's hard enough to remember my sales and inventory turnover from last month. Why should I clutter my brain and my hard drive with this new version of Trivial Pursuit?"

Because it establishes you as an effective listener, that's why. Effective listeners remember order dates and quality specifications. They are easier to talk with when there's a problem with a shipment. In short, effective listeners sell more customers ... and keep them longer.

For 50-plus years at MackayMitchell Envelope, we have used a device to get people to record and review this kind of data. It's a questionnaire form. People inside our company have taken to calling it the "Mackay 66" (because it has 66 questions). We complete at least one on every customer. It lists all the vital statistics we gather, such as our contact's educational background, career history, family, special interests, and life-style. It's continually updated and it's studied to death in our company. Our overriding goal is to know more about our customers than they know about themselves.

I've had people ask me, "Don't you feel like the FBI or the KGB, running dossiers on your customers?" I don't. The questionnaire is merely a system for organizing what the best executives and salespeople have done for a long time: demonstrate exceptional understanding of their customers as people.

The point here is that people don't care how much you know about them once they realize how much you care about them. One purpose of the Mackay 66 is to empower the perceptive and empathetic salesperson with information that, channeled properly, produces a response that says, "I care."

For example, question number 48 asks about the customer's vacation habits. These say a lot about people. Is he the outdoors type who loves to whitewater raft on the Colorado or camp out at Yosemite? Does she like to tour Europe and Japan by bus? Is she a tennis enthusiast who plans her vacations around major professional tournaments? How would that lover of the outdoors react to a book of photographs of Yosemite by Ansel Adams? What would the sightseeing type say on receiving an array of hard-to-get brochures of unusual and exotic tours? Imagine the reaction of that tennis buff as she reads previews of Wimbledon and the U.S. Open we sent her a few weeks before those events.

Each of these instances happened. The donor wasn't a husband, wife, friend, or neighbor but a MackayMitchell account executive. Were these gestures perceived as insincere? They could have been, but they weren't. They represented actions taken after seller and buyer had achieved a certain level of communication and rapport. The best salespeople are "other conscious." They're sensitive people who are genuinely interested in others. They don't do things to people; they do things for people, after they've learned something about those people.

> *People don't care how much*
> *you know about them once they realize*
> *how much you care about them.*

Who were the sources of information regarding the vacation habits? They could have been assistants, receptionists, or other suppliers. They often are. In these situations, however, they were the prospective customers themselves. The information about vacations was cross-referenced to question number 51, "conversational interests." In each instance, this information was culled from the customer over breakfast or lunch (naturally, after the name of the customer's favorite restaurant was elicited from the assistant).

When the little gift came, it arrived on the prospective customer's birthday (the date is asked in question number 5), long after that introductory lunch or breakfast. Was the customer aware that the giver had an ulterior motive? Yes, in part. But what also came across was the salesperson's thoughtfulness and sincere desire to establish a solid, long-term relationship. The personal touch is so rare a commodity today, it becomes a standout. Does it always translate into new business? Not always, but often; and not always immediately, but eventually.

I learned the impact of using one's intelligence on customers when, as a young constituent, I walked into Senator Hubert Humphrey's Washington office for the first time and he amazed me by showing he knew about my goals and avocations. Although we had only a brief conversation, his genuine likability and superior information turned me into a friend, a supporter, and a loyal contributor. The intent is not to get something on somebody. The goal is to pay attention to the person across the table. Salespeople sell to people, not computer screens. I have found that salespeople who can't understand and empathize with the goals of the people they sell to are incapable of understanding and empathizing with the goals of the broader organization they later have to serve in filling the order.

At any big social function you see effective top executives creating mental profiles on the people they meet. Leaders learn to pay attention to what's important in other people's lives. That means keeping your antennae up and noticing the details. It's not manipulation but disarmament. All of us are naturally hostile to persuasion and salesmanship. Well, everyone whose livelihood relies on making a sale had better learn to neutralize that hostility, so he or she can get on with the business of honestly selling the product. Our format simplifies the method and puts it into the hands of the little guy. With practice and a modicum of discipline, anyone can master the skill of harvesting customer awareness.

Once each year, our marketing people and our top operating people sit down and review the material on our key customers, with special emphasis on the last page—the point that deals with the customer's view of the goals and issues facing that company's management, as stated to our salespeople. This analysis of common customer issues is the launching pad for our planning.

When a salesperson quits or retires, it is very difficult to sustain valuable personal relationships in business-to-business selling. But these continually updated files have allowed us to put a new client contact into position far faster than most businesses can. The greatest danger when you lose a veteran salesperson is, of course, that the client will be spirited away too. The documentation that the salesperson has built up, (often over years) gives us a big edge in establishing a lasting relationship between the new MackayMitchell account representative and the customer.

Ask the salespeople in any company, "Are you dealing with the same purchasing agent at Jones & Smith today as you were five years ago?" The answer is quite probably no. In international businesses especially, purchasing people are transferred often. Therefore, make a point of getting to know the whole department—especially the up-and-comers—and learn the company's practices on moving people. In short, dig your well before you're thirsty.

As a manager, I judge the intensity and the discipline of our 35-plus salespeople by looking at how up-to-date their customer profiles are. Scanning the profile is stage one of any account review. Sometimes a superficially completed profile or one filled with awkward hedges is a godsend of an early warning. It can signal a salesperson mismatch with an account. And that means a switch in account assignments before the customer decides to take a hike.

As important as the questionnaire is, it's vital not to confuse the form with the mind-set and discipline it represents. The form is just a tool to readjust people's vision. You and I have both sat across the table from too many salespeople whose eyes became glazed over with indifference, whose sighs of boredom betrayed their thought, which was: "Just sign the order, you're wasting my time"– as if you, the customer, were obligated to help boost the caller's profits. The method built around the questionnaire arms the seller with superior information and intelligence and inspires a positive attitude toward making the sale.

> *The customer relationship is like a marriage:*
> *Small shows of sensitivity and awareness*
> *maintain spice.*

A salesperson never has to make a cold call. Ever. Granted, you aren't likely to learn much about family background and career history until you actually have your first meeting, but there is no reason you can't become an instant expert on a prospect company in advance. The Internet has revolutionized access to information. The Internet has become the greatest library the world could ever imagine. One of the best research investments you can make is to sit down with your IT people for a couple of hours and learn how to effectively search information on industry segments, customers, suppliers and even former employees.

Ask your friendly banker. "Isn't that breaching a confidence?" you ask. Not if your banker doesn't happen to be your customer's banker too. Then there's the chamber of commerce buyer's guide. (Every chamber has one.) You can do a Google search to monitor the local and trade press. The list of easily available background sources is nearly endless.

This research requires the same skills that went into writing a good term paper. But so few people think of applying these disciplines in a sales situation. So many people close the door on their education and training and don't even think of using in real life what they spent dozens of years learning. The best business recruits recognize that their real education doesn't begin until they enter the workplace—because then education becomes application. I constantly remind my people that knowledge doesn't become power until it's used. That's why we use the Mackay 66. That's why we write it all down.

In 50-plus years of selling, I have never called on a buyer I haven't sold. In that I'm not exceptional. The diligence and perseverance of our company's selling strategy are, however, unusual. Hardly anyone ever makes a sale on the first call. That's just as true for us as anyone else. Not every lead qualifies as a legitimate prospect. But when we decide that we want a company's envelope business, we've ultimately made the sale in virtually every case.

Years ago, as the business was building, I (as CEO) made the first call on most major prospects, and that call was invariably brief. I asked for 300 seconds of my counterpart's time, and usually the meeting lasted no more than 180 seconds. "We very much want to be your supplier," I'd say. "It means a lot to us. Here's what we can do …" My comments were confined to differentiators like price, quality, service, or delivery time—whatever distinguished us from the competing supplier.

Courtship & Marriage

Many CEOs were terrific salespeople at early stages of their careers. But too often, after being installed in carpeted corner offices at headquarters, they have allowed a distance to grow between themselves and the sales arena. Then the CEO's only selling involvement takes place behind closed doors, pitching the board on a strategic plan or the executive committee on a management succession scenario.

That's a big mistake. Salespeople need to see the top people out there, mixing it up, setting the example. That's a prime reason why some of America's most visible chief executives are so effective when they get out in public to pitch their products on national television.

They're not just selling products. They're also motivating their people to sell the products. Selling chickens may not be the most pleasant job in the world, but if the boss thinks it's important enough to do himself, then maybe it's important for the chicken salesperson too.

Most initial contacts are lengthy presentations with glowing claims concocted for audiences that are often too large and too highly placed. They abuse the customer's time. You don't need a Wagnerian epic to communicate a persuasive message. After all, the Gettysburg Address has only 270 words and the Lord's Prayer, a mere 54.

The follow-up happens on the technical level. What the CEO as salesperson should be selling is not product. It is a strategic idea . . . and it is trust.

The relationship is just like a marriage: small shows of sensitivity and awareness keep the spice in it. We have one customer whose version of heaven is salmon fishing in Scotland. You can bet that at least once a year an article on salmon angling from a fine British sporting magazine shows up on his desk, together with a handwritten note. A prospective customer, whom we have pursued for a year and a half, makes a pilgrimage to New York twice a year to feast on operas and concerts. Each September this client receives, in a MackayMitchell envelope, the Carnegie Hall and Lincoln

Center season programs. The personal touch is noticeably changing his attitude toward us.

I remember when we had a customer who was a University of Michigan alumnus and a passionate Wolverine football fan. In 1986, Michigan won the Big Ten football title. My assistant found out where Rose Bowl programs were being printed, ordered a copy, and had it sent to him. He was unable to attend the game on New Year's Day, but I'm sure he sat in front of his living room TV with that program clutched in his hands.

It takes time. Strategic, humanized selling always does. It is also based on very self-evident precepts ... astonishingly simple. As the Prussian strategist Karl von Clausewitz wrote in *On War*: "Everything in strategy is very simple, but that does not mean everything is very easy."

Care & feeding of salespeople

The stereotype of the huckster who cajoles his mark into resigned submission—that portrait is one for the business history books. Today's seller must understand modern communication styles and concepts. That begins with knowing when to close one's mouth and open one's ears, but it entails a whole lot more.

Before we hire a salesperson, I always socialize with the candidate and the spouse. Too many important deals are secured in a social setting, like the ballpark or the ballet, for the candidate's ease in handling contacts to be ignored. It's also important to see a candidate in his or her home setting. Is what you find at all like what you were told it would be? That is, is this person a straight shooter or prone to exaggeration? You don't want to learn later that a decade-long customer has been victimized by overpromises. I make a point of having a long telephone conversation with the candidate and sprinkling it with awkward pauses just to see how he or she handles them. Given the amount of business transacted by phone these days, you had better find out if you're signing up Ellen DeGeneres or Homer Simpson.

We send our salespeople through Dale Carnegie or Toastmasters training because these courses emphasize how important listening is to effective speaking. Any outstanding public speaker will tell you that a speech is nothing more or less than the sale of an idea. The best speakers anchor their skills by monitoring audience feedback, from body language to the cough count.

Our constant exposure to electronic media has changed the way we expect to be persuaded. Persuaders must get to the point faster, speak in a vivid and engaging way, and blend their pitches so cleverly with customized information that it never sounds like mere patter.

An entire industry, insurance, has been built on the Law of Large Numbers. There are 300+ million living Americans. The insurance people can predict within one-fourth of 1% how many of us will die within the next 12 months. They can tell us where, and how, in what age bracket, and of what sex, race, and profession. The only thing they can't predict is who. The sales force must apply this same principle to its prospect lists. If the lists are long enough, there will be salespeople for #1 suppliers who retire or die, or lose their territories for a hundred other reasons.

What you can't predict is which of your competitors will succumb to the Law of Large Numbers. But fortunately, as in the insurance business, which one doesn't matter. All that matters is that your salespeople have the perseverance and patience to position your company as #2 to enough prospects. If they're standing second in line in enough lines, sooner or later they will move up to #1.

In our company, we recognize that the kind of dogged persistence and patience it takes to convert a #2 position to a #1 position is very tough for the typical salesperson to master. By nature, salespeople tend to be more like racehorses than plow horses. The instant gratification syndrome that gets a salesperson to the finish line first is an ingrained part of the salesperson's makeup. That's why we insist on the customer profiles, the follow-ups, the disciplined account review, and most of all, the emphasis on human sensitivity. Doubtless, it is not the fanciest marketing management system, but it is uncommonly effective for managing salespeople.

Let me illustrate by passing on a conversation I had with a young salesperson named Phil. It was like a lot of talks I've had with my salespeople over the years. Phil came into my office looking agitated.

Phil: Mr. Mackay, I need your help. I've been wrestling for over a year now to get the account at International Transom, and it's just no use. I think I'd better give up.

Mackay: (motions him toward a chair): They buy from Enveloping Envelope, don't they?

Phil (sits): Yes, for seven years, and they don't have the slightest interest in changing suppliers. I think it's time for me to write off this particular prospect and spend my time on business with greater promise.

By making ourselves #2 in many places, sooner or later we'll be #1 in some.

Mackay: International Transom is a very attractive account, Phil. I wonder if you're not chasing the wrong goal. Accept for now that they're happy with EE. Your objective isn't to become their supplier overnight; it's to become the undisputed holder of second place. (Phil looks skeptical, so Mackay proceeds to explain the Law of Large Numbers.)

Phil (gloomily): Based on what I've seen in calling on Bystrom, the purchasing agent at International Transom, it's going to be a long wait.

Mackay: I see you've got the customer's profile there. Let me take a look. (Phil hands him the folder. Mackay reads it.) Aha. Just as I thought. This questionnaire reads like a dry and pretty spotty profile on someone you find intimidating, if not a little hostile. There's no vitality, no real grasp of the customer or his motivation. It's lifeless.

Phil (agitated again): But this guy is a clam, not at all outgoing.

Mackay (sternly): Did you read his desk? Were there any mementos there that told you something about him? How about plaques on the wall? What's his alma mater? If he's businesslike with you, what are his aspirations? How does he identify with company goals? You don't have in here a recent article or current analyst's report on this company. (Arises from his desk and gesticulates as he paces to and fro.) How well have you shown him that you know and admire his company? That you know how it fits in its industry?

Do you know the strengths and weaknesses of Enveloping Envelope in terms of International Transom? Have you emphasized to Bystrom those strengths that MackayMitchell has almost exclusively, like centralized imprinting?

Phil: Well, I ...

Mackay: Have you, in short, made Bystrom feel absolutely terrible about not buying from you right now? Terrible because you are so knowledgeable, aware, interested in him as a person, and representing a company that is clearly differentiated from EE in important and positive ways?

Phil (looking more excited now than upset): I see what you mean, Mr. Mackay. You're asking me to aspire to the #2 position, if we can't be first. Instead of telling me to win, you're telling me to prepare to win.

Mackay (patting Phil on the back as they move toward the office door): Exactly, Phil. (He beams at Phil.) You've got the right idea.

It wasn't long before Phil's folder on his prospect sharpened and its byte count fattened considerably. In this he had a lot of help, by the way, from others at MackayMitchell Envelope who knew International Transom, Bystrom, and Enveloping Envelope. We have a reward system that recognizes outstanding individual performers and reinforces collaborative behavior. We don't focus on just the top salesperson. Each month we also reward the best networking that leads to a sale. We recognize a salesperson whose persistence has paid off with substantial new business. We spotlight a salesperson whose customer or competitive insight produced a significant change in the way we do business.

Your selling strategy

My definition of a great salesperson is not someone who can get the order. Anyone can get the order if he or she is willing to make enough promises about price or delivery time or service. A great salesperson is someone who can get the order—and the reorder—from a prospect who is already doing business with someone else. No salespeople can aspire to that kind of selling unless they are prepared to think strategically and humanistically about their customers. The beauty of it is, though, that with patience and some simple tools, you don't have to be a strategic genius or a management psychologist to excel.

If, however, you are a CEO or a manager who determines the climate and attitudes in your company, then I counsel you strongly to ensure that selling and salespeople in your organization get proper leadership and the recognition they deserve. No matter how many strides you make in product quality or asset management or new design features, there is no tool more likely to harm or help your market share than your selling strategy. This is a lesson companies can learn on their own initiative . . . or, I have no doubt, they will learn at the hands of their competitors.

Conclusion

When good things happen to me, I'm often tempted to believe there's something magical about them ... and maybe there is. But I'm not about to sit back passively and wait for the magic to kick in. I want to give it every possible opportunity to happen.

For years I had a plaque on the wall that read as follows: "Pray for a good harvest ... but keep on hoeing!" I looked at that so many times over the years that it's permanently burned into my memory.

If you want your CMS to produce a fruitful harvest, you have to be persistent and you have to keep on hoeing. Remember:

1. **It's a chronicle of your life**. As the world changes, one thing will remain constant—the relationships you develop over a lifetime.

2. **Always keep your antennae up**. Don't forget the most important skill that nobody teaches. It's networking.

3. **Consider it an investment**. We all start out in life with the same amount of time in each day. It's what we do with it that counts.

4. **Remembering doesn't work**. He who counts on his memory has a fool for a filing system.

5. **You have to give a piece of your mind to get peace of mind**. You can utilize the insight and vision of your whole network to help you "see around corners."

6. **Make it work for you, not against you**. With your CMS, only two things count: it's fun, and it works.

7. **Make connections the old-fashioned way**. You don't have to know everything. Seek out people who know the things you don't.

8. **Unlock the secrets of the universe**. Give them what they expect, then "wow" them with the unexpected.

9. **You can improve on human nature**. With practice, using your CMS becomes more than a discipline, it's a way of life.

10. **Never say no for the other guy**. Your next great opportunity is there, somewhere, buried in your CMS, just waiting for you to find it.

The greatest joy of my contact management system is knowing I can make the world a smaller, friendlier place by reaching out to the network of people I've gotten to know over the years. It has changed my life ... and I guarantee it will change yours.

Appendix I

Self-Test: How Good Are Your Network Building Skills?

Answer these questions and rate yourself on a 1-5 scale, 1 being not true and 5 being very true:

1. I have a large network of people I can call upon when I need help, information, or a resource.   1 2 3 4 5

2. When I meet someone new, I record and file information about that person within 24 hours.   1 2 3 4 5

3. I add somebody new to my CMS at least every week.   1 2 3 4 5

4. I follow up with new contacts right away— writing a note, e-mail, making a phone call, or forwarding a pertinent article.   1 2 3 4 5

5. I keep track of special things that matter to my contacts like their family, hobbies and achievements.   1 2 3 4 5

6. I can easily find out when I was last in contact with someone.   1 2 3 4 5

7. When I mail or e-mail something—a resumé, sales letter, change of address—I can count on having correct name spellings, titles, addresses for everyone in my network.   1 2 3 4 5

8. I know about and acknowledge special dates like birthdays, anniversaries and graduations.   1 2 3 4 5

9. When I want to give a business gift, I can count on my CMS to provide me with an excellent idea of what the person might like.   1 2 3 4 5

10. I make it easy for others to add me to their network by providing my business card, notifying them of address changes, and informing them about my career progress.   1 2 3 4 5

11. When friends ask me for the name of a good resource, I have no trouble providing one.   1 2 3 4 5

12. When the moment comes, I can really "wow" a customer, prospect or potential employer with special information or an idea that shows I care.   1 2 3 4 5

Total the points above and score yourself:

0–24   You are in rough shape. It is time to
       make a change.

25–36 You are doing some things right.
       Now get to work.

37–44 You are off to a great start. Build on what you
       have done so far.

45–55 You have got superstar potential.
       All you need is the polish.

56–60 You are already there. Keep up the great effort!

Appendix II

Essential Information
For Your Contact Management System

1. **Name**. This one is obvious, but you should include any nicknames or casual forms of address that you or your office staff will use in correspondence.

2. **Title**. Keep this up to date for use in correspondence, and it's a good idea to acknowledge promotions and job changes as soon as you hear of them.

3. **Company**. I'm amazed at how many letters I receive that have my name and/or my company's name spelled incorrectly. Being sloppy about such personal details is the best way to ruin a first impression.

4. **Address**. Make sure that you have every address your contact can provide: street addresses for office and home, e-mail, Twitter, LinkedIn, Facebook or whatever medium you can use to reach the person. Keep your CMS up to date with any address changes. Sending a short "Congratulations on your new office!" note is a great way to keep in touch, and sends the message that you are well-organized.

5. **Phone numbers**. All of them: office direct line, home, cell, company switchboard, and assistant's direct

line. Is there a good time of day to call? Does a text or e-mail get a better response than a phone call?

6. **Birthdate and Place**. I'm a stickler for keeping track of birthdays, and I like to know where people were born because it tells me a lot about them. One of the most successful people I know always seemed unap-proachable until I found out he came from a tiny town of 800 people on the Iron Range in Minnesota, near the town where my mother was born.

7. **Connections**. This is the place to jog your memory as to where you met someone, who introduced you, what activity you shared, and when you last saw one another. As the years go by, these old connections can be invaluable.

8. **Family**. Family information about people in your network is important for you to know because it's so important to *them*. I include items about spouses and children, as well as their activities, whenever possible.

9. **Education**. Educational background is something many people feel strongly about. As National President of the University of Minnesota Alumni Association, I was constantly amazed by the level of commitment and enthusiasm exhibited by alumni members. Even decades after graduation, they continued to feel intensely con-nected to the place where they began their adult lives.

10. **Affiliations**. This includes memberships in professional organizations, churches, clubs, political groups, etc. I've met people all over the world and developed some wonderful friendships based simply on our mutual membership in an organization. It's a great conversation starter and gives otherwise busy people a good excuse to stay in touch.

11. **Special Interests**. Here I try to record what Joseph Campbell refers to as a person's "bliss"—that is whatever, besides work, makes a person really light up. I recently discovered that one of my old friends is fascinated with space exploration and I sent him some articles about the Hubble Telescope. You would have thought I'd sent him a million dollars.

12. **Significant Career History**. This includes brief notes on anything you want to remember about someone's career, such as a big promotion, a lay-off in his or her company, or the name of a former employer.

13. **Accomplishments**. I love keeping track of awards, publications, promotions and achievements of people I care about because I know how much effort went into them.

14. **Wow**. This is a space I leave for recording any tidbit of information that could make our next meet-

ing unforgettable. Little things mean so much to most people. On a recent trip to Stockholm, I picked up that day's newspaper (in Swedish, of course) for a transplanted Swedish friend living in Minneapolis. He often reads them online, but was delighted to receive the print version from across the ocean.

Appendix III

The Two-Minute Drill

I could fill volumes about chance meetings that have changed people's lives, led to jobs, business opportunities, partnerships, new ideas, all just because people sought other people with similar interests.

But the secret is to seek them out.

The two-minute drill can help.

I did this two-minute drill for the first time in my hometown of Minneapolis in the early '90s with 1,000 people in the audience. Within two weeks, I'd gotten over 35 letters and cards telling me that thanks to the drill they're now either doing business with the person they met or have a high probability of doing business with them. 35 cards. And I'd bet there were plenty of others who struck oil but didn't bother to write. This exercise is meaningful because almost invariably my mail tells me that it really jump starts the habit of networking.

Here's how the drill works:

I ask the audience to look around and ask someone they don't know to be their partner. When the whistle blows, they have two minutes to tell that person everything about themselves that they regard as worth telling. A total of two minutes for background, achievement, hopes, dreams, goals, hobbies, marriage, children, frustrations over the Cubs' pennant chances—everything they can think of.

When the two minutes are up, the whistle blows again, and the switch is on. It's amazing what you can learn about another person in just two minutes.

I'll be out of their lives and back home on my deck before the day is over. But the person they just met might be in their lives forever.

Remember how you played the dating game? You cruised. You schmoozed. You perused. You worked out. You went to beaches and ballgames and concerts and singles bars. You went to places you'd never be caught dead in today. Why? To meet new people.

Well, why stop now? I'm sure your partner is truly wonderful, but he or she—and his and her many, many equally wonderful friends, associates and relatives—are not the last people in the world you will ever want to meet.

You know how it's done. You've proved it. You've done it before and you've succeeded. Keep at it. Turn off that tube. Get out amongst them. It can change your life. Volunteer work. Political clubs. Hobby groups. Service clubs. Church groups. Industry associations. Extension courses. The internet. The outernet . . . whatever.

And remember this the next time you attend a seminar or speech: The person next to you, or in front of you, or behind you, is much more important than the person at the front of the room.

The point is, never, never pass up an opportunity to meet new people. By doing your own "two-minute drill" once a day, you'll meet at least 365 new contacts in just a year's time. Isn't that worth a two-minute investment?

If you have thoughts, comments, or ideas about this book, I'd love to hear from you. (Please, no requests for personal advice.) Write to me at the following address:

Harvey Mackay
MackayMitchell Envelope Company
2100 Elm Street Southeast
Minneapolis, MN 55414
www.harveymackay.com

Notes

Notes

Notes